Overcoming Your Pathological Gambling

Overcoming Your Pathological Gambling

Overcoming Your Pathological Gambling

Workbook

Robert Ladouceur • Stella Lachance

UNIVERSITY PRESS

2007

OXFORD
UNIVERSITY PRESS

Oxford University Press, Inc., publishes works that further
Oxford University's objective of excellence
in research, scholarship, and education.

Oxford   New York
Auckland   Cape Town   Dar es Salaam   Hong Kong   Karachi
Kuala Lumpur   Madrid   Melbourne   Mexico City   Nairobi
New Delhi   Shanghai   Taipei   Toronto

With offices in
Argentina   Austria   Brazil   Chile   Czech Republic   France   Greece
Guatemala   Hungary   Italy   Japan   Poland   Portugal   Singapore
South Korea   Switzerland   Thailand   Turkey   Ukraine   Vietnam

Copyright © 2007 by Oxford University Press, Inc.

Published by Oxford University Press, Inc.
198 Madison Avenue, New York, New York 10016

www.oup.com

Oxford is a registered trademark of Oxford University Press

ISBN-13 978-0-19-531701-5
ISBN 0-19-531701-7

Printed in the United States of America
on acid-free paper

About Treatments*ThatWork*™

One of the most difficult problems confronting patients with various disorders and diseases is finding the best help available. Everyone is aware of friends or family who have sought treatment from a seemingly reputable practitioner, only to find out later from another doctor that the original diagnosis was wrong or the treatments recommended were inappropriate or perhaps even harmful. Most patients, or family members, address this problem by reading everything they can about their symptoms, seeking information on the Internet, or aggressively "asking around" to tap knowledge from friends and acquaintances. Governments and healthcare policymakers are also aware that people in need don't always get the best treatments—something they refer to as "variability in healthcare practices."

Now healthcare systems around the world are attempting to correct this variability by introducing "evidence-based practice." This simply means that it is in everyone's interest that patients get the most up-to-date and effective care for a particular problem. Healthcare policymakers have also recognized that it is very useful to give consumers of healthcare as much information as possible, so that they can make intelligent decisions in a collaborative effort to improve health and mental health. This series, Treatments *That Work*™, is designed to accomplish just that. Only the latest and most effective interventions for particular problems are described, in user-friendly language. To be included in this series, each treatment program must pass the highest standards of evidence available, as determined by a scientific advisory board. Thus, when individuals with these problems, or their family members, seek an expert clinician who is familiar with these interventions and decides that they are appropriate, they will have confidence that they are receiving the best care available. Of course, only your healthcare professional can decide on the right mix of treatments for you.

This particular program presents the latest version of a cognitive-behavioral treatment for pathological gambling.

David H. Barlow, Editor-in-Chief,
Treatments *ThatWork*™
Boston, Massachusetts

Contents

Chapter 1   *Introduction*

Goals

▣ To learn about pathological gambling

▣ To learn about this treatment program and what it will involve

What Is Pathological Gambling?

Pathological gambling is characterized by a loss of control over gambling, deception about the extent of involvement with gambling, family and job disruption, theft, and chasing losses (American Psychiatric Association [APA], 1994).

Diagnostic Criteria for Pathological Gambling

The characteristics and criteria defining pathological gambling are described in the *Diagnostic and Statistical Manual of Mental Disorders* (*DSM-IV-TR*), which is published by the APA. Pathological gambling is listed under "Impulse control disorders not elsewhere classified" and is defined as persistent and recurrent maladaptive gambling that interferes with personal, family, or occupational functioning. The 10 criteria established by the APA (APA, 1994) can be used to obtain precious information regarding gambling-related behaviors, as well as the severity of gambling habits. Furthermore, examination of the gambling problem according to these criteria shed light on the consequences of gambling in different spheres of gamblers' lives: family, occupational, social, academic, financial, and legal. Note that at least 5 of the 10 criteria listed below must be met for a diagnosis of pathological gambling.

1. The gambler is preoccupied with gambling (e.g., preoccupied with reliving past gambling experiences, handicapping or planning the next venture, or thinking of ways to get money with which to gamble).

2. The gambler needs to gamble with increasing amounts of money in order to achieve the desired excitement.

3. The gambler has had repeated unsuccessful efforts to control, cut back, or stop gambling.

4. The gambler is restless or irritable when attempting to cut back or stop gambling.

5. The gambler gambles as a way of escaping from problems or of relieving a dysphoric mood (e.g., feelings of helplessness, guilt, anxiety, depression).

6. After losing money gambling, the gambler often returns another day to get even (i.e., "chasing" one's losses).

7. The gambler lies to family members, his therapist, or others to conceal the extent of involvement with gambling.

8. The gambler has committed illegal acts such as forgery, fraud, theft, or embezzlement to finance gambling.

9. The gambler has jeopardized or lost a significant relationship, job, or educational or career opportunity because of gambling.

10. The gambler relies on others to provide money to relieve a desperate financial situation caused by gambling.

Brief Description of the Program

This program is based on the concepts of cognitive-behavioral therapy (CBT). It will help you to understand all aspects of your gambling problem, as well as teach you ways to stop gambling and also how to deal with the consequences of your gambling behavior. The primary goal of treatment is to help you completely abstain from gambling.

Over the past 10 years, we have studied the basic psychology of gambling. The crucial finding was that the majority of gamblers hold erroneous thoughts concerning the outcome of the game. Many believe gambling is a game of skill and that they can control the outcome by adopting different strategies. During treatment, you will learn to recognize errors in your thinking that keep you gambling, while also learning to correct them.

Throughout this program, you will be required to complete various exercises and worksheets. These tools will help you to acquire and develop the skills you need to counter your desire to gamble in your daily life. These exercises will also assist you in mastering difficult situations where you may be tempted to gamble.

Steps of the Program

Pretreatment assessment

Treatment (approximately 12 sessions)

Session 1

Motivational enhancement

Sessions 2 and 3

Behavioral interventions:

Chain of behaviors linked to excessive gambling

High-risk situations

Behavioral strategies to adopt

Sessions 4 to 10

Cognitive interventions:

Analysis of a gambling session

Definition of chance

Importance of the inner dialogue

Presentation of the gambling traps

Awareness to erroneous cognitions

Recognition and modification of erroneous cognitions

Sessions 11 and 12

Relapse prevention

Posttreatment assessment

Follow-ups

Using This Workbook

This workbook contains all the forms, worksheets, and exercises you will need to participate in this treatment program. You will move through this book under the direction of your therapist. Each chapter includes a list of goals and is focused on specific methods or techniques to help you assess your problem, understand it, and modify your thoughts, feelings, and behaviors. Interactive forms and worksheets are included in each chapter where they are introduced. Additional copies can be downloaded from the Treatments *ThatWork*™ Web site at www.oup.com/us/ttw. Follow your therapist's instructions for use of these forms. Homework exercises are listed at the end of each chapter and will be assigned by your therapist.

Chapter 2   *Pretreatment Assessment*

Goals

- To complete assessment questionnaires

Pretreatment Assessment

Before officially beginning this program, your therapist will want to work with you to complete several different assessment measures. A detailed assessment enables your therapist to determine the severity of your gambling problem with regard to frequency and intensity, while taking into account the consequences you and those around you have experienced because of your gambling. Furthermore, pretreatment assessment is a necessary step for your therapist to tailor a treatment plan that fits with your specific needs.

The Diagnostic Interview for Pathological Gambling

Your therapist will begin your assessment by asking you a number of questions from the Diagnostic Interview for Pathological Gambling (DIPG). This questionnaire will help both you and your therapist determine whether you meet the criteria for pathological gambling.

Gambling-Related Questions

The five questions on page 6 help your therapist to quickly obtain information regarding your desire to gamble in the past week, the number of times you gambled, the time spent gambling, as well as the amount of money spent gambling during the last week.

You will complete this exercise during your session.

Gambling-Related Questions

For questions 1 and 2, circle the number that corresponds to the way that you have felt over the past week.

Perceived Control

1. To what extent do you feel that your gambling problem is resolved or under control?

0 ----- 10 ----- 20 ----- 30 ----- 40 ----- 50 ----- 60 ----- 70 ----- 80 ----- 90 ----- 100%

| Not at all resolved | A little | Moderately | A lot | Totally resolved |

Urge to Gamble

2. To what extent have you felt the urge to gamble in the past week?

0 ----- 10 ----- 20 ----- 30 ----- 40 ----- 50 ----- 60 ----- 70 ----- 80 ----- 90 ----- 100%

| Not at all | A little | Moderately | A lot | Totally |

Gambling Frequency

3. How many times have you gambled in the past week? _____

4. How much time (hours and minutes) have you spent gambling during the past week? _____

5. How much money have you wagered during the past week? _____

Perceived Self-Efficacy Questionnaire

You will describe the situations you consider the most risky for you and then estimate the extent to which you believe you are able to resist the urge to gamble if you find yourself in one of these situations. The exercise on page 7 will allow your therapist to determine which situations need to be tended to and to create a behavioral intervention plan adapted to your needs.

Conclusion

Your therapist will go over the results of your assessments with you. Together you will determine your goals for treatment. Your therapist may want to further explore some of the material you brought up. This phase is important.

Perceived Self-Efficacy Questionnaire

Please describe your high-risk situations for gambling excessively (for example: "when I am bored and have nothing to do" or "when I just had an argument with my boss"). Then, indicate on a scale of 0 to 10 your level of confidence in controlling your gambling habits if you faced these situations at the present time.

Situation 1

_____

_____

_____

If you had to face this situation at the present time, to what extent would you have confidence in controlling your gambling habits?

0 ------- 1 ------- 2 ------- 3 ------- 4 ------- 5 ------- 6 ------- 7 ------- 8 ------- 9 ------- 10

   Not at all   A little   Moderately   A lot   Totally

Situation 2

_____

_____

_____

If you had to face this situation at the present time, to what extent would you have confidence in controlling your gambling habits?

0 ------- 1 ------- 2 ------- 3 ------- 4 ------- 5 ------- 6 ------- 7 ------- 8 ------- 9 ------- 10

   Not at all   A little   Moderately   A lot   Totally

Situation 3

_____

_____

_____

If you had to face this situation at the present time, to what extent would you have confidence in controlling your gambling habits?

0 ------- 1 ------- 2 ------- 3 ------- 4 ------- 5 ------- 6 ------- 7 ------- 8 ------- 9 ------- 10

   Not at all   A little   Moderately   A lot   Totally

Chapter 3   *Session 1*

Goals

- To enhance your motivation to change

- To clarify your treatment goals

  In this session, and throughout the rest of the treatment program, you will need to work to keep your motivation high. High motivation is key to success. Work with your therapist to complete the Advantages and Disadvantage exercise on page 10. This will help you to see the negative effects that gambling has on your life. This worksheet will also help you to realize the benefits of stopping gambling.

Why Do You Gamble and Why Do You Want to Stop?

The three exercises on pages 11–13 will help you think more closely about the reasons why you gamble in the first place, and why you want to change your behavior.

Your Treatment Goals

The two exercises on pages 14 and 15 are designed to help you become aware of how much gambling occupies your life. At this stage, gambling takes up a large part of your time, energy, and financial resources. You are likely ignoring, or at least paying less attention to, other areas of your life, like work and family. The first pie chart included here will show you just how big a part gambling plays in your life right now. After completing it, fill out the second chart and visualize how much you want gambling to be represented at the end of treatment.

Advantages and Disadvantages

POSITIVE ASPECTS OF GAMBLING (the benefits that gambling gives me)	NEGATIVE ASPECTS OF STOPPING GAMBLING (what I lose if I stop gambling)

NEGATIVE CONSEQUENCES OF GAMBLING (current and potential for the future)	ADVANTAGES OF STOPPING GAMBLING (what I gain if I stop gambling)
Current: Potential:	

What I Like About Gambling

What I Hate About Gambling

Here Are the Reasons Why I Want to Stop Gambling

Using this circle, create a "pie chart" to indicate the portion of your life currently taken up by:

- gambling

- your work

- your family

- your other leisure activities

- your social life

- other priorities (list) _____

_____

_____

_____

Gambling's Place in My Life at the End of Treatment

Using this circle, create a "pie chart" to indicate the portion of your life you would like to be taken up by each of these at the *end of treatment.*

- gambling

- your work

- your family

- your other leisure activities

- your social life

- other priorities (list—include new ones if you like) _____

_____

_____

_____

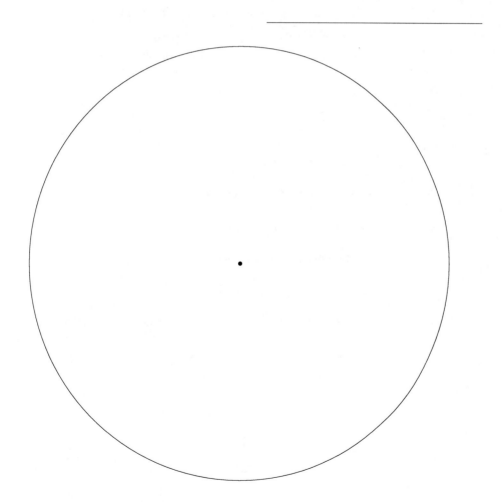

A central part of this program is record-keeping or daily monitoring. Sometimes, it is hard for a gambler to acknowledge the full extent of his or her gambling problem. Keeping a daily record of your gambling activities will help you become conscious of your problem. It will quantify the intensity of your desire to gamble and the large sums of money you have lost. The Daily Self-Monitoring Diary on the following page enables you to monitor your progress throughout treatment. As time goes on, you will be able to see the changes that take place and the progress you're making.

Use the diary every day to rate how in control you felt of your gambling, as well as your desire to gamble, on a scale from 0 to 100. Indicate the number of times you gambled during each day, the number of hours you spent gambling, and the amount of money you lost. Write about the feelings you had throughout the day and any event that may have provoked your urge to gamble. Since you will complete a diary on a daily basis, you may photocopy the sample included here or download multiple copies at the Treatments *That Work*™ Web site at www.oup.com/us/ttw.

Homework

Complete the following exercises:

- ✎ What I Like About Gambling
- ✎ What I Hate About Gambling
- ✎ Here Are the Reasons Why I Want to Stop Gambling
- ✎ Gambling's Place in My Life Today
- ✎ Gambling's Place in My Life at the End of Treatment

Begin using the Daily Self-Monitoring Diary and complete one each day from now to the next session.

Daily Self-Monitoring Diary

Date:

	/ /	/ /	/ /	/ /	/ /	/ /	/ /
1. To what extent do I perceive that my gambling problem is under control? 0---10---20---30---40---50---60---70---80---90---100 not at all a little moderately very much completely							
2. What is my desire to gamble today? 0---10---20---30---40---50---60---70---80---90---100 nonexistent weak average high very high							
3. To what extent do I perceive myself as being able to abstain from gambling? 0---10---20---30---40---50---60---70---80---90---100 not at all a little moderately very much completely							
4. Did I gamble today?							
5. How much time (hours & minutes) did I spend gambling?							
6. How much money did I spend on gambling, excluding wins?							
7. Specify your state of mind or the particular events of the day.							

Chapter 4   *Sessions 2 & 3*

Goals

- To understand the chain of events that leads to excessive gambling, and the importance of high-risk situations in this chain

- To increase your awareness of high-risk situations

- To help you identify concrete strategies that can be used to avoid high-risk situations

- To learn the five steps to effective problem-solving

Risky Situations

Over the next two sessions with your therapist, you will work to identify high-risk situations in which you are more than likely to gamble and to learn strategies for abstaining from gambling in these situations. A high-risk situation is the first step in the chain that leads to heavy gambling (Fig. 4.1).

Risky situations can be divided into the following categories: exposure to gambling, financial situation, relationship problems, free time, and consuming alcohol or drugs.

Exposure to Gambling

Being in a gambling establishment obviously represents an important risky situation. If you persistently frequent these places, you repeatedly foster your desire to gamble and make it difficult to resist. We understand that it is unrealistic to think that you can continually avoid gambling games, given their increasing availability and accessibility. However, did you know that you can voluntarily bar yourself from gaming establishments?

Certain casinos offer a program that allows gamblers to ban themselves from the establishment. In these self-exclusion programs, the gambler meets with the establishment's security service and signs a self-exclusion form.

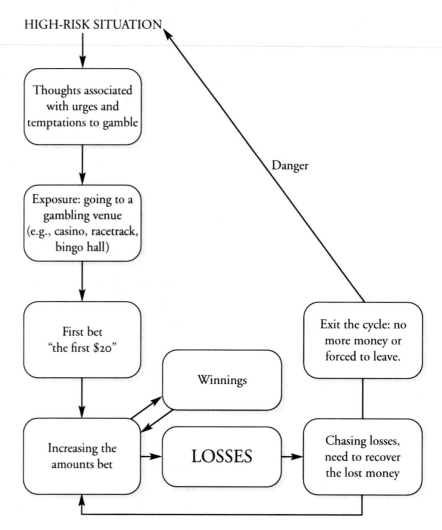

HIGH-RISK SITUATION

Thoughts associated with urges and temptations to gamble

Exposure: going to a gambling venue (e.g., casino, racetrack, bingo hall)

First bet "the first $20"

Increasing the amounts bet

Winnings

LOSSES

Exit the cycle: no more money or forced to leave.

Chasing losses, need to recover the lost money

Danger

Figure 4.1
Problem Gambling Behavioral Chain

The gambler's photo is also taken so that security can identify him or her if he or she tries to enter the establishment again. The duration of self-exclusion varies according to the gambler's request and the norms in place within the casino. Certain contracts last a few months, while others extend over several years.

If the places where you gamble do not offer this type of program, you can arrange to meet with the managers of the establishment to explain your problem and ask that they don't let you in. If you find it impossible to self-exclude from certain places, you should expect to confront numerous situations that risk you being exposed to gambling.

Your therapist will discuss with you in more detail the following strategies for dealing with these situations.

Finding Oneself Near a Gambling Establishment

Many gamblers report that they most often gamble after work. If this applies to you, try the following suggestions:

- Change your route and ensure that the gambling establishment is not on your way home from work.

- Systematically avoid going to places where it is possible for you to gamble.

Finding Oneself in a Gambling Establishment

If you find yourself in a gambling establishment despite your attempts to avoid it, your therapist may propose that you do the following:

- Remain as far as possible from the video lottery terminals or the counter where lottery tickets are sold.

- Avoid asking personnel or other clients about the output of video lottery terminals, the results of lottery drawings, or the results of any other form of gambling game.

Finding Oneself Alone in a Gambling Establishment

For certain gamblers, the problem is not so much being in a gambling establishment as it is going to one alone. You may find that you can go out to bars with friends without being tempted to gamble. When you are alone, however, you may feel a strong desire to gamble and be likelier to succumb to it. In this case, we suggest that you never go to gambling places alone.

Receiving an Invitation to Gamble

Receiving an invitation to go to a gambling establishment represents another risky situation that deserves consideration. If you find it difficult to refuse these invitations, your therapist will work with you to:

- Learn to assert yourself and develop strategies to refuse such offers.

- Discuss your gambling problem with friends and family, and tell them that you are in the process of dealing with this difficulty. Let them know that they should avoid inviting you out to gambling establishments. If the majority of your friends are linked, closely or not, to your gambling activities, it is justifiable to make changes to certain relationships or to question them.

Financial Situation

In addition to avoiding being exposed to gambling, you should restrict your access to money as much as possible. You can temporarily transfer the management of your money to a loved one or a third person, or engage the services of a financial consultant.

You may find it embarrassing to give control of your finances to someone else, but you will realize that in the short term, a little embarrassment is better than the risk of losing it all.

You can discuss with your therapist the possibility of hiring a financial consultant or an organization to teach you how to establish a budget according to your revenues and current expenses. Together, you and your consultant can assess your financial situation and decide what actions to take. If you settle your financial situation, you will be less preoccupied by the idea of gambling to make money and will be in a better position to continue with this program.

What to Do When You Have Money

There are other ways you can deal with your financial situation if you can't bring yourself to allow someone else to handle your money. Try to carry only a limited amount of pocket money with you. You can also try not keeping any cash on you at all. Here are some suggestions for restricting access to your money:

- Cancel your credit cards.

- Avoid the ATM and don't get a bank card.

- Limit access to your bank account by requesting that a co-signature be required for all cash withdrawals.

- Give clear instructions to friends, family, and owners of gambling establishments that they are not to lend you any money.

If you receive a regular paycheck, or if you sometimes receive an inflow of money from other sources, you can:

- Sign up for direct deposit with your company.

- Have a close friend or relative accompany you when you deposit money into your bank account.

- Give your paycheck to your spouse or other trusted person.

- Plan the payday scenario in advance: plan all of the day's activities and each movement in detail.

- Warn a friend or relative of the next arrival of money and discuss solutions.

- Give another person the responsibility of picking up the mail so as not to be in direct contact with checks or bills received.

What to Do When You Don't Have Money

Lack of money is as risky a situation as is access to money. There are several risky situations that are directly linked to a lack of financial resources. Here are a few:

- Lacking money to pay for rent, food, and clothing

- Receiving a bill

- Having lost the evening before

- Wanting to buy a birthday present for a loved one

- Being invited to an outing or a leisure activity and not having enough money to participate

How can you decrease this financial stress? Simply through communication: you must discuss your gambling problem with friends and family.

Relationship Difficulties

Often, pathological gambling leads to a deterioration of the gambler's social network. Certain of your relationships may have ended because of your gambling. Now that you have decided to stop gambling, you may likely face isolation and loneliness. Your therapist will help you to progressively resume contact with your friends and family. Do not hesitate to express your feelings on this issue. What is your goal? How would you go about solving this problem? Ask your therapist to help you out.

Lack of Occupations and Activities

Once you stop gambling, you will find that all of a sudden you have a lot of free time that you must occupy. What were your activities and interests before gambling took up all of your time? Do you have any passions or hobbies? As gambling became increasingly important in your life, you likely neglected or completely abandoned other activities that you once found pleasurable. You may find it relatively easy to find new pastimes and to resume the activities you gave up. Keeping yourself active avoids periods of idleness during which you are likely to be flooded with thoughts about gambling.

If you have always used gambling to fill a void and don't really have an idea of where to start in terms of getting involved with other activities and pastimes, your therapist will help you to make a list of activities (new or otherwise) that are accessible and that are likely to interest you. Your list should include activities that you can do alone, as well as those that require the presence of other people.

Consuming Alcohol or Drugs

Consuming alcohol or drugs can greatly reduce your willpower to resist gambling. The effects of alcohol can impair your perception and prevent you from becoming aware of the seriousness of beginning or continuing to gamble. We strongly encourage you to decrease your consumption of alcohol or drugs while participating in this program.

My High-Risk Situations

Use the following checklist to identify the situations where your urge to gamble is particularly intense.

According to your own experience, would you say that you tend to gamble heavily:

when you expose yourself to gambling? ☐

when you are low on/out of money? ☐

when you are experiencing relationship difficulties? ☐

when you consume alcohol or drugs? ☐

when you have no other activities to do and feel bored? ☐

when you have to deal with daily problems and unpleasant emotions
(e.g., frustration, feeling of failure, sadness, disappointment)? ☐

Daily Problems (Frustration, Failure, Rejection)

Certain gamblers experience difficulties that are not specific to gambling, and these problems can cause the gambler to relapse. An inability to deal with daily problems and a lack of problem-solving skills can lead to a desire to escape.

The problems that we refer to here can take on diverse forms. They are difficulties or events in our daily lives, from problems at work to situations of conflict at home. Clearly, we speak of any problematic situation that leads to anger, frustration, sadness, or discouragement.

You can use the problem-solving steps and the problem-solving exercise found at the end of this chapter to deal with any of the difficulties you face in your daily life. Your therapist will discuss these in more detail with you.

Knowing the high-risk situations that apply to you allows you to develop strategies to address them. The two most effective strategies are *avoidance* and *management*. In some cases, you can easily avoid risks (for example, drinking alcohol before you gamble), while others are more difficult to get around (no one is beyond experiencing problems with other people, for example). It is therefore very important to learn to deal with high-risk situations you cannot avoid. This is what you will learn to do, with the help of your therapist.

Strategies to Help Avoid High-Risk Situations

Here is a list of strategies that many people use to help control their gambling habits. Read them carefully and decide those that might work for you.

1. Strategies to avoid unwanted exposure to gambling
    - Avoid being near places where you can gamble outside your designated hours.
    - Change your route to ensure that a gambling venue is not on your way.
    - Avoid asking the staff or other clients how the slots are paying out, about lottery results, or about results from any other form of gambling.
    - Avoid being alone in a gambling venue.

2. Strategies to improve your financial situation
    - Restrict your access to money (cash, credit, and ATMs).
    - Temporarily assign the management of your finances to a significant other.
    - Ask a significant other to manage your deposits and payments.
    - Get help from a credit counselor or an agency that can help you with your budget.
    - Learn how to develop a budget that fits your income and expenses.
    - Make firm plans to pay off your debts (starting with the most urgent).

- Keep very little money on you (strict minimum).
- Cancel your credit cards.
- Cut up your debit cards.
- Designate a co-signer for your bank withdrawals.
- Give a clear message to friends and family not to give you personal loans.
- Arrange for an automatic deposit for your paycheck.
- Take someone with you when making bank deposits.
- Hand your paychecks over to someone you trust.
- Plan non-gambling activities around payday.
- Inform a significant other about incoming money (e.g., income tax refund).
- Ask someone else to get the mail in order to limit your access to checks and income.

3. Strategies to work out relationships with others
- Identify a significant person (e.g., parent, work colleague) who has strong assertive and communication skills, and take the time to observe and learn from that person.
- Participate in Gamblers Anonymous (GA).
- Join a new leisure, educational, or recreational activity.

4. Strategies to control the effects of alcohol or drugs on your gambling
- Drink only nonalcoholic beverages when you are in a gambling venue.
- Stay at home or at a friend's when you want to drink alcohol.
- When you go to gambling venues, always go with someone who knows that your gambling problem is linked with alcohol or drug use.

5. Strategies to help with boredom
- Find some new stimulating activities (off-road cycling, in-line skating).
- Do some volunteer work.
- Play games of skill (e.g., billiards [without gambling!], golf).
- Make a detailed schedule to help yourself with time management and with your activities.

Dealing With My High-Risk Situations

In the spaces below, describe the high-risk situations that affect you the most, and indicate how you might deal with them.

A.   Situation 1: _____

_____

_____

My strategy: _____

_____

_____

_____

B.   Situation 2: _____

_____

_____

My strategy: _____

_____

_____

_____

C.   Situation 3: _____

_____

_____

My strategy: _____

_____

_____

_____

D.   Situation 4: _____

_____

_____

My strategy: _____

_____

_____

_____

E.   Situation 5: _____

_____

_____

My strategy: _____

_____

_____

_____

F.   Situation 6: _____

_____

_____

My strategy: _____

_____

_____

_____

G.   Situation 7: _____

_____

_____

My strategy: _____

_____

_____

_____

1. Clearly Identify the Problem/Stop and Think

Give yourself time to reflect on the problem so that you avoid impulsive reactions. Pausing allows you to clearly identify what the problem is. Spending enough time defining a problem often gives better answers in the end. This is not always easy, especially when we are dealing with the consequences of the problem. At such times, it can be useful to ask yourself the following questions:

- "What is it about this situation that I do not like?"

- "What exactly needs to change?"

- "What do I want?"

- "What is my goal? What would it look like if the problem were no longer here?"

- "What are the obstacles?"

- "What prevents me from attaining my goal?"

Another approach is to "begin with the end in mind." Imagine you got up one morning and the problem was no longer there. How would you know it was gone? What would be different? How would people act differently? Paint a picture of your world without the problem, and ask yourself what changes you can make that might move you in that direction. In this context, a change involves doing something differently, or thinking about something in a different way. Any change you adopt has the potential to affect the problem in a positive way.

2. List Different Possible Solutions

There are a number of ways to address any problem. To begin the process of identifying answers, list as many possible solutions (i.e., changes that you can make) as you can without judging or evaluating their potential effectiveness. The more possible solutions you can generate, the more likely you are to solve the problem and overcome the related obstacles. Here are some questions that can help to frame possible solutions:

- "What can I do to resolve this problem?"

■ "How can I react? What can I do differently?"

■ "What can I tell myself? Is there a more constructive way to interpret the situation?"

At this stage, do not eliminate any solution because it seems impossible at first glance. Later, if seen in another light, it could offer some advantage.

3. Assess Each Possibility

Before selecting your preferred solution, spend some more time evaluating the ones that seem more promising. For each of these possible solutions, explore the potential consequences using the following questions:

■ "What will happen if I decide to do this? What will change?"

■ "What are the advantages of this choice? How will it reduce the problem?"

■ "What are the disadvantages of this choice? What might go wrong?"

Again, we suggest that you write out the answers. This helps you state your answers in a more thoughtful way and will make it easier to select your final course of action.

4. Choose a Solution

You are now at the stage of making a choice. Review your statement of the problem and the various promising solutions you have written out. Select the one that appears to offer the best positive impact. This, in theory, will be the one that serves you the best. You will now need to test it in the real world.

5. Experiment With the Chosen Solution

If you give your solution a trial run and the results are satisfactory, excellent! If they do not have the expected effects, however, you will need to go back to your list of possible solutions. Choose another that might avoid the problems you encountered with the first, and give it a trial run, just as you did the first time. Continue to experiment in this way until you achieve a satisfactory result.

Here are some tips to consider as you strive to solve problems and make things better:

▪ Consider enlisting a family member or a friend to help implement your solution. Explain that you are trying to fix things and that his or her support or contribution could increase your chances for success.

▪ Accept that it is sometimes possible only to reduce a problem, and not eliminate it altogether. When this happens, it is still progress and moves you in the direction you want to go.

▪ On occasion, give things a bit of time to come around. Problems often take quite a while to develop, and so will turning them around.

To conclude, there is no miracle solution or perfect solution to any given problem. However, these steps offer a model that can help you solve some of the difficulties that have developed. At first, you may need to get familiar with this approach, but over time, you will notice that the more you have gone through the steps, the less time it will take. They will give you time to stop and think about the situations you face and to make effective decisions for you and your significant others.

Homework

Complete the following exercises:

✎ My High-Risk Situations

✎ Strategies to Help Me Avoid High-Risk Situations

✎ Dealing With My High-Risk Situations

✎ Five Steps for Problem-Solving (optional)

Continue to complete the Daily Self-Monitoring Diary.

Five Steps for Problem-Solving

Until you become familiar with this approach, we recommend that you take the time to write out each step of your problem-solving action plan. You may photocopy this exercise from the book or download multiple copies at the Treatments *That Work*™ Web site at www.oup.com/us/ttw.

1. Identify clearly the problem/stop and think:

   What is going on? Give details—try answering whichever of the following questions apply to the situation you are addressing.

   What is the problem? _____

   _____

   _____

   _____

   _____

   With whom do I have a conflict? _____

   _____

   _____

   _____

   _____

   What do I dislike about the situation? _____

   _____

   _____

   _____

   _____

   Exactly what must change? _____

   _____

   _____

   _____

   _____

continued

What is my goal? _____

_____

_____

_____

_____

What are the obstacles? _____

_____

_____

_____

_____

2. List possible solutions:

Be uncritical at this stage—list all solutions you can think of. In this context, a solution is a change that you can make. Changes most often include doing something differently (e.g., reacting in a different way) and thinking about something in a different way. Introducing changes to what you currently do will also change what happens, often for the better. Ask yourself the following questions to help come up with answers:

What can I do to solve this problem? _____

_____

_____

_____

_____

How can I act/react in a different way? _____

_____

_____

_____

_____

What could I think about in a different way? _____

_____

_____

_____

_____

3.   Evaluate each possibility:

Which solution appears most promising? What will happen if I decide to apply it? What are the advantages of this choice? Describe the disadvantages of each choice, and grade it with a code (+++, ++, +, -, –, —, X) to help sort things out.

Option 1: _____

_____

_____

_____

_____

Option 2: _____

_____

_____

_____

_____

Option 3: _____

_____

_____

_____

_____

Option 4: _____

_____

_____

_____

_____

Option 5: _____

_____

_____

_____

_____

4. Choose a solution:

    Review your assessments and scores, and select the most promising option(s) to try.
    Here is/are the selected solution(s):

    _____

    _____

    _____

    _____

5. Try out the solution you have selected:

    Here are the results or the effectiveness of trying out my solution, along with my comments: _____

    _____

    _____

    _____

    _____

    _____

If the solution you have selected does not give the expected results, go back to step 3 and consider another option.

Chapter 5   *Session 4*

Goals

▨ To discuss in detail your most recent gambling session

▨ To identify the erroneous thoughts that you had before, during, and after the gambling session

Analyzing a Gambling Session

During this session, your therapist will ask you to imagine your last gambling experience and will ask you numerous questions about it. This exercise will help you to realize the errors in your thinking that led you to gamble at that time. Remember, one of the main goals of this program is to help you change your erroneous thoughts about gambling. In order to change your thoughts, you have to recognize them first.

Talk with your therapist about the context, the places, the people, the events, or any other element that has a close or more distant relationship to the gambling session you are discussing. Be specific and give as many details as possible about your decisions, actions, and any events that occurred while gambling. Talk about amounts wagered, and describe or explain changes in your betting style or strategy, the different choices made, and decisions taken regarding the game. Discuss your reactions following a win or a loss. Focus on what happened after the gambling session, and express what you felt at the end of the gambling session and in the hours that followed. Your therapist will guide you through this exercise.

Homework

✎ Continue applying strategies to avoid/manage high-risk situations.

✎ If needed, continue practicing problem-solving skills.

Continue to complete the Daily Self-Monitoring Diary.

Chapter 6   *Sessions 5–7*

Goals

- To understand the concept of chance and the difference between games of chance and games of skill

- To become aware of your inner dialogue regarding gambling

- To explore the influence of this inner dialogue on your decisions to gamble

- To review a range of gambling traps and learn to recognize erroneous thoughts

What Is Chance?

- Chance means that the outcome of an event is *impossible to predict.*

- Chance also means that it is *impossible to control the outcome* of the event.

Because of these characteristics, there is no way of knowing when you will win, or if you will win, at a game of chance.

Games of Chance vs. Games of Skill

Games of chance are those in which mathematical calculation or the ability of the player has no part in determining the outcome. Examples include 6/49, Super 7, Bingo (including e-Bingo), instant lotteries ("scratch and win"), slot machines, and roulette.

Games of skill are those in which the player's ability has, or is likely to have, some influence on the outcome. Examples include billiards, golf, archery, hockey, badminton, and tennis.

The situation	Two thoughts; two interpretations	Two reactions
I am walking down the street and I see someone I know well. She doesn't wave or say hello.	1. I feel that she avoided me, that she pretended not to see me.	She is so impolite! This is no way to treat people...that's the last time I talk to her!
	2. I feel that she is deep in thought about something. She's probably distracted and didn't see me.	I hope nothing serious has happened to her.

Figure 6.1

Two interpretations of the same situation = two different reactions

The Importance of Our Thoughts and Perceptions on How We React to Situations

To understand how we interpret situations, see Figure 6.1, which presents two different interpretations of the same situation. Once you understand this process, we will then introduce how the perception of a game may determine how we cope with this gambling activity.

Your Inner Dialogue

Because it is not always possible to avoid high-risk situations, you must learn how to deal with situations that are unavoidable and unpredictable. Focusing on the thoughts or "inner dialogue" you have during high-risk situations is the first step in developing new skills needed to effectively manage them.

Your therapist will introduce the ABCD model to you. A completed example is shown in Figure 6.2. A blank exercise is also included on page 42. You may photocopy the exercise from this book or download multiple copies at the Treatments *ThatWork*™ Web site at www.oup.com/us/ttw.

A High-Risk Situation	B Automatic Thought That Leads to Gambling More Than I Planned	C Behavior	D Consequence
I get my paycheck	I tell myself I can gamble a small part of this money and come out ahead.	I gamble more and spend more than I planned to. I end up losing much more than I can afford.	I feel upset and guilty. I don't have enough money and will have to do without for the rest of the week.

Figure 6.2

Example of completed ABCD Exercise

ABCD Model

The ABCD model works in the following way: (A) **high-risk situations** generate (B) **thoughts** that lay the foundations for (C) **behavior** in the form of gambling. This behavior, should it involve spending more time or money than planned, will result in one or more (D) **consequences.** Consequences can be either positive or negative, and you are trying to eliminate the negative ones by stopping or cutting back on your gambling. Note also that some consequences are immediate and others are more long term. Positive consequences tend to be more immediate, while negative ones may appear immediately or after a while, and very often extend over the longer term.

At this stage, move your focus to the notion of **choice.** Through the ABCD Exercise included on page 42, you will recognize some of the thoughts that were behind your choice to gamble when you found yourself in a high-risk situation. It is these thoughts that led you to gamble. If these thoughts did not occur, or if they were intercepted, then gambling would not have followed.

The Gambling Traps

In the heat of gambling, it is common to feel that your chances of winning are almost certain. You hope to beat the odds and hit the jackpot, and winning is all you are focused on. This is the precise point where emotion takes

ABCD Exercise—Your Turn

A High-Risk Situation	B Automatic Thought That Leads to Gambling More Than I Planned	C Behavior	D Consequence

over from reason and sells you on the idea that your turn to win is about to come. And once this idea takes hold, you continue to bet more and more.

This reading reviews some of the thoughts and ideas that lie behind such emotions. They are usually false and are known as "gambling traps" because they cause you to lose much more than you planned to or can afford.

To begin with, it is important to understand the difference between emotions when you are *not* gambling as opposed to emotions when you *are*.

When you are not gambling, you are emotionally detached and in what is known as a "cold" situation. Your thoughts tend to be more realistic and more accurately reflect how luck or chance can work against you. But when the desire to gamble strikes, you become emotionally aroused and move into a "hot" situation. This is when you are likely to fall into emotional and mental traps, and when you most need to resist thoughts saying that you are likely to win.

By understanding the emotional and mental traps that are part of gambling, you will gain powerful tools to protect yourself from heavy losses.

What Is Chance?

The first step is to understand the true meaning of luck or "chance." Chance is something that you cannot *predict* or *control*. This means that:

■ You cannot *foresee* the outcome, and

■ You cannot *control or influence* the outcome.

In games of *skill* (such as golf, darts, soccer, or hockey), the results depend very much on the amount of effort and perseverance you invest. And you can improve through practice: the more you practice, the better you become, very often making you better than someone who doesn't practice.

In games of *chance*, it is impossible to develop or improve winning strategies or to influence outcomes. There simply are no skills involved, and so there is no way to improve your skills or make you better than anyone else. Whenever anyone does win, it is only as a result of chance.

Casinos and slots venues *only* offer games of chance (although they may be disguised as games of skill). For example, even though you are allowed to choose your number when playing roulette, it is impossible to control or predict where the ball will stop. This same reality also applies to slot machines: no "ability" is required other than putting in money and pressing the button. You have no control over the outcome, despite design features that give you "choices" and encourage you to believe otherwise.

Why You Can't Improve in Games of Chance

There are two main reasons why gamblers think they can improve their chances of winning. First, they believe that outcomes (winning or losing) are somehow linked to previous results. Second, they believe there are things they can do to improve their odds. The following sections show why both beliefs are completely false and how they form the basis for gambling problems.

Rule 1: The Independence of Outcomes

All games of chance operate within an absolute law known as the "independence of outcomes." This means that each play is a separate "event" and is in no way influenced by earlier plays or events—that is, it is *independent* of all previous outcomes.

Our first inclination before engaging in any form of gambling is to watch and look for patterns. It is natural to assume that studying something will reveal strategies that can improve our chances of winning. The truth is, however, that observation only lets us see things that are not there; all strategies are completely useless. The reason why is illustrated by the "red marble experiment."

A single red marble is set among a thousand white ones in a bin (much like those in lottery drawings that can be turned by a handle on the side). The task is to close your eyes, select a marble from the bin, and bet on your chances of selecting the red marble. If you select a white marble, you lose. *You then have to put it back into the bin,* which is well stirred by turning the handle a few times, and try again.

Imagine now that you have drawn 50 times in a row, and on each attempt you drew a white marble. After these 50 unsuccessful attempts, are you due (or more likely) to pick the red marble on the 51st draw? The answer, of course, is "no."

This type of gambling is known as a *replacement draw*. Every white marble that is drawn is put back into the bucket. Before your first draw, your chances of picking the red marble were 1,000 to 1. When you put the first white marble you drew back in the bin (and stirred it well to mix them all up again), you *reset the game* to 1,000-to-1 odds again. You can see how you *always* have one chance in a thousand of winning. Even after betting 50, 100, or 300 times, you are no "closer" to selecting the red marble than you were the very first time. And, let's face it, the chances of picking the red marble in 1,000-to-1 odds are pretty slim, as every gambling provider knows.

Applying the Facts

The hard facts are that the number of attempts and your history of losing in no way influence your chances of winning on any try. This is what "independence of outcomes" means.

"What if I draw 1,000 times?" you might ask. "Am I likely to win?" Again, the answer is not what you would hope for. In a replacement draw, the odds are that you would have to draw many more than a thousand times before you are likely to get your first win. Try it with some friends: get a bag and place 19 white marbles and 1 red one in it. Let each person draw, and then put the selected marble back in the bag. Shake it and let someone draw again. Record how many draws are made versus the number of wins in this replacement draw with "fabulous" odds of only 20 to 1! You will be dismayed to learn that 20-to-1 odds in no way means that someone wins every 20 draws.

Now let's apply this information to the slots. As you know, players often vary how quickly they play, the amount they bet, the precise moment they push the button, and so on. The red marble experiment shows us that whether you make 300 draws quickly or slowly, vary the amount you bet on each draw, or close your eyes waiting for an inspired moment to make your draw in no way alters your chances of winning.

The "independence of outcomes" means:

- It is impossible to predict (or correctly anticipate) any outcome.

- Your chances of winning get no better as you increase your number of bets.

- Each play is a completely new game.

- The probability of winning always remains the same.

Bottom line: you *never* "get closer" to winning.

Recognizing Traps

Gambling venues *only* offer games of chance. In so doing, they ensure that the law of independence of outcomes always applies, and you can never improve your performance.

Gambling traps occur when people's thoughts take over and tell them it is somehow possible to improve their chances. Very often, such thoughts lead to betting more money that was planned or could be afforded. They are the paths to *impaired control* and gambling problems.

Here are some direct quotes showing how gamblers overlook the independence of outcomes and fall into traps:

- "At roulette, you are in a better position after three even numbers come up in a row. This means that a series of odd numbers are due soon."

- "At roulette, I bet the same number all night long. I start by looking at the summary table and choose one that hasn't come up in a long time. Then, I stick with it: each loss means the likelihood of it coming up gets nearer!"

- "It is better to find out how a slot machine has done during the day. Playing a machine that hasn't paid out all day is a smart strategy!"

- "When the blackjack dealer has been lucky many times in a row, I increase the amount of my bet because he is due to lose."

At the slots, many players believe it's preferable to change machines after five or six plays if it doesn't pay out. Thinking this way suggests two possibilities:

- The machine keeps track of the bets and past payouts in order to "decide" it's time for the next payout.

- Wins are determined in advance and put on a "conveyor belt"— each losing play moves the next win one step closer, and winning is just a matter of persevering.

But as we now know, both "theories" are completely wrong and are traps. Think back to the red marble experiment. The marbles don't keep track of your losses and "decide" they'll push the red one into your hand (possibility 1 above). Nor are slots like gumball machines, where the foil-wrapped winner gets closer to the delivery chute with each loss (possibility 2 above).

With replacement draws, each play is independent of all past ones, and winning is *all about* chance. Also, keep in mind that your chances in any game are so small that you can never count on them.

These facts mean that every dollar spent over your limit is almost a guaranteed loss.

Rule 2: Illusions of Control

A second critical fact in regaining control over your gambling is to recognize that you have no control over chance, and nothing you do will increase your chances of winning. Believing you can influence a gambling outcome is known as an "illusion of control." The following sections review common illusions of control for different games.

Slot Machines Illusions

Slot machines are designed to create illusions of control. Although all have similar electronics on the inside, each presents a different "face" to the player. This is where subtle traps are put in to create illusions of control. The designer's skill is reflected in how difficult it is to resist the illusion.

For each play, the slot machine simply draws a random number using an electronic generator, and the outcome is coded as either a win (large or small) or a loss. This means that a random outcome is selected every time you press the play button. By pressing the button, all you do is generate the random number and reveal the outcome.

The amount you wager can alter the size of the potential pot but has no impact on the probability of winning. When you choose to press the button has no impact. Nor does it serve any purpose to vary the amount you bet, hoping this will influence the programming of the machine. Regardless of any actions you take, the probability of winning on any play is the same.

At the slots, it's an illusion to think that you can increase your chances by:

- Observing a machine's cycles or *patterns* of winning or losing

- Choosing a machine by the amount paid out that day, as if there are "full" or "empty" machines

- Choosing a slot machine that just took another player's money

- "Testing" the machine with small initial bets

- Pressing the button at a specific moment or betting on a preferred machine

- Changing bets or machines if the machine doesn't pay

- Letting the machine "rest" by changing games

- Pressing the start button in different ways (e.g., changing your level of force, hitting it repeatedly, or changing your speed of betting)

- Cashing in (or not) and believing either action might affect future outcomes

- Betting more heavily when the machine is "starting to pay out"

- Returning to the same machine the next day, having lost the night before

- Calculating in your mind the number of bets made, the time, and so forth

- Observing payouts at nearby machines in order to decide the amount you bet

- Using *any* trick, strategy, or system

Lottery Illusions

Although relatively inoffensive, lotteries promote a range of illusions of control. Common examples are to think you can increase your chances of winning by:

- Choosing numbers such as birthdays

- Keeping track of winning numbers from previous drawings

- Keeping the same numbers from drawing to drawing

- Betting on lucky numbers

- Placing numbers evenly on the betting form

- Varying where tickets are purchased

- Studying winning patterns of sports teams

Bingo Illusions

At bingo, common illusions are to think you can increase your chances of winning by:

- Choosing cards that have your favorite numbers on them

- Marking numbers in a certain way

- Choosing a table where nobody has won in a while

- Choosing a table where several people have won recently

- Not playing cards with certain numbers on them

- Going to play with someone you consider to be lucky

Blackjack Illusions

At blackjack, there is no better strategy than to follow the basic rules known to all players. Any other strategy puts you at a disadvantage in the long run. With this in mind, you really have no decisions to make, and it is an illusion to think you can increase your chances of winning by:

- Trying to memorize or count cards

- Taking the time to choose a particular table, seat, or dealer

- Observing the cards dealt to other players in order to decide whether to draw another of your own

- Observing the style of other players before starting to play

- Slowing or speeding up the pace of the game

- Placing very high bets

Roulette Illusions

The arrangement of the numbers inside the roulette wheel can inspire thoughts about control, and introducing the croupier into the equation allows for even more. The rolling of the ball encourages you to observe the croupier's technique in hopes of better predicting the outcome.

At roulette, it is an illusion to think you can increase your chances of winning by:

- Observing the croupier's rolling technique (e.g., rhythm, regularity, continuity)

- Choosing a particular table, seat, or croupier

- Watching previous rolls and keeping count of outcomes

- Betting on "lucky" numbers

- Watching a player who is winning and placing similar bets

- Increasing the size of your bet if the ball stops close to your preferred numbers

Horse Racing Illusions

Research has shown that experienced horse gamblers ("handicappers") achieve the same level of payout as rookies. The bottom line is that despite studying an impressive amount of statistical information, they lose just as much as someone who selects horses on a random basis. Yet, they are considered "specialists," even though their financial situations often turn out to be disastrous.

Horse betters embrace a range of illusions, each implying that chance is a predictable and logical "science." They are convinced that their skills improve with time and study and that experience plays in their favor. Many such "experts" dream of earning a living within their chosen "science."

When betting on the horses, it is an illusion to think you can increase your chances of winning by:

- Studying statistics from previous races

- Calculating future race times from a horse's previous times

- Playing the "rebound"—a horse that paid out terribly will do better in the next

- Assessing the race distance, the track condition, or type of surface (grass or dirt)

- Analyzing the physical attributes of the horse (e.g., muscularity, way of standing)

Superstitions

Superstitions are ritualistic, magical, or "sacred" thoughts and actions believed to have the power to overcome chance. They tap into gamblers' strong desires to win and mark a transition into mysticism in the effort to predict wins.

Here are quotes for common gambling-related superstitions:

- "The 21st of the month is lucky, as it is made up of three times the number seven."

- "I start to win immediately after eating a cheese sandwich. I know it sounds odd, but it works all the time!"

- "When I don't try to win, I do. Wanting to win undermines my luck and makes me lose. I need to pull back on desire and get into the zone."

Conclusion

At this point, you can appreciate that if you do not counter erroneous thoughts, particularly when you are emotionally aroused by the desire to gamble (i.e., in a "hot" situation), you are more likely to incur substantial losses.

Failing to control these thoughts allows you to develop a false feeling of personal effectiveness, and to believe that all the time and money invested in gambling is bound to be rewarded one day. By maintaining these false beliefs, you lay the foundations for impaired control, problem gambling, and harm to your health, social, and financial well-being.

My Own Traps

Based on the reading you have just completed, describe on pages 53–56 the traps you have already fallen into.

Homework

✎ Review the concept of chance and the differences between games of chance and games of skill.

✎ Review the section on the importance of our thoughts and perceptions.

✎ Complete the ABCD Exercise.

✎ Read "The Gambling Traps."

✎ Complete My Own Traps exercise.

✎ Continue applying strategies to avoid/manage high-risk situations.

✎ If needed, continue practicing problem-solving skills.

Continue to complete the Daily Self-Monitoring Diary.

My Traps: Slot Machines

Trap 1: _____

_____

_____

_____

_____

Trap 2: _____

_____

_____

_____

_____

Trap 3: _____

_____

_____

_____

_____

Trap 4: _____

_____

_____

_____

_____

Trap 5: _____

_____

_____

_____

Trap 6: _____

_____

_____

_____

_____

My Traps: Bingo

Trap 1: _____

_____

_____

_____

Trap 2: _____

_____

_____

_____

Trap 3: _____

_____

_____

_____

Trap 4: _____

_____

_____

_____

Trap 5: _____

_____

_____

_____

Trap 6: _____

_____

_____

_____

My Traps: Horse Racing

Trap 1: _____

_____

_____

_____

Trap 2: _____

_____

_____

_____

Trap 3: _____

_____

_____

_____

Trap 4: _____

_____

_____

_____

Trap 5: _____

_____

_____

_____

Trap 6: _____

_____

_____

_____

My Traps: Lottery Tickets

Trap 1: _____

_____

_____

_____

Trap 2: _____

_____

_____

_____

Trap 3: _____

_____

_____

_____

Trap 4: _____

_____

_____

_____

Trap 5: _____

_____

_____

_____

Trap 6: _____

_____

_____

_____

Chapter 7

Sessions 8–10

Goals

- To recognize the erroneous cognitions that affect your gambling

- To develop skills for challenging and casting doubt on the erroneous thoughts that lead to excessive gambling

- To understand and realize that you have the power to decide to gamble or not

Challenging Your Erroneous Thoughts

Challenging erroneous thoughts is the essence of the entire therapeutic process. In these next few sessions, you will work at modifying spontaneous thoughts that cause you to gamble or that encourage you to continue gambling. The practical exercises you will complete at this point in the program allow you to organize your thoughts and to act upon them. The more you complete these exercises, the more you become capable of resisting your desire to gamble. You will learn to no longer let yourself be trapped by risky situations and by the erroneous ideas they provoke.

At the beginning of each of these sessions, you will relate the occasions where you managed to abstain from gambling despite a strong impulse otherwise. Little by little you will realize that you have the power to rebel against your desire to gamble.

It's My Call

The It's My Call exercise on page 59 promotes recognition and integration of the relationship between thoughts and the decision whether to gamble

High-Risk Situation	Automatic Thoughts That Lead to Gambling More Than Planned	New Thoughts That Let Me Control My Gambling	Behavior: The Course of Action I Choose	Outcome
I'm at home. I'm alone. My husband is working. I know he won't be back until late.	I could go for a few minutes and try a $20 bet just to check if I'm lucky today.	Let's be honest. I know that if I gamble $20 and I lose it right away, I will continue to put money in the machine, to chase my money back. And if I gamble $20 and win, I will gamble it all.	I'll take advantage of my husband being out to rent a "chick flick." He hates romantic comedies.	I'm so happy with myself. It has been a while since I've done something that enjoyable. I'm glad I decided not to surrender to my initial thought.

Figure 7.1

Example of completed It's My Call exercise

or not. The objective of the exercise is to discover and modify your spontaneous thoughts, which form the basis of the decision to gamble.

Complete the exercise based on a recent relapse episode or from one of your high-risk situations. Take each of your erroneous thoughts and replace them with more accurate ones that reflect the realities of gambling and that are in line with your goal to stop gambling. Write down the new ideas in the column representing thoughts that give you control over your desire to gamble.

Over the next few sessions your therapist will review your completed exercises with you. You will complete as many exercises as there are times when you have felt the urge to gamble or have faced a risky situation. You may photocopy the exercise from this book or download multiple copies from the Treatments *ThatWork*™ Web site at www.oup.com/us/ttw.

A completed example of the exercise is shown in Figure 7.1.

It's My Call Exercise

High-Risk Situation	Automatic Thoughts That Lead to Gambling More Than Planned	New Thoughts That Let Me Control My Gambling	Behavior: The Course of Action I Choose	Outcome

✎ Complete an It's My Call exercise every time you experience the urge to gamble or face a risky situation.

✎ Continue applying strategies to avoid/manage high-risk situations.

✎ If needed, continue practicing problem-solving skills.

Continue to complete the Daily Self-Monitoring Diary.

Chapter 8   *Sessions 11 & 12*

Goals

- To understand relapse as a normal process

- To realize the possibility of a slip or relapse

- To develop strategies that will help to prevent slips or a relapse

- To establish what to do in case of a slip or relapse and discuss emergency measures to take

Understanding Relapse

Relapse can be defined a number of ways. For some, a relapse means a return to old gambling habits. For others, gambling only once in a while corresponds to relapse. According to us, relapse is a return to a gambling cycle or a loss of control in a gambling situation. Keep in mind that relapse is an integral part of a normal recovery process. Relapse is *not* an automatic sentence to a lifetime of problem gambling, and although relapse is common with addiction, it is preventable.

Throughout this program, you have worked long and hard to develop effective coping responses to deal with high-risk situations. Having this skill decreases the probability of relapse significantly. Each time you are able to deal effectively with a high-risk situation, you will feel more confident in your ability to abstain from gambling. You will experience a sense of increased control over your gambling behavior. As time goes on, you will find it easier and easier to resist the urge to gamble.

Relapse Prevention: Sophie's Relapse

Sophie has been on a diet for the past 4 months and has lost 20 pounds. To achieve this goal, she had to modify her eating habits and start exercising regularly. These 4 months have not always been easy and have required many sacrifices, but Sophie is proud of the results. She feels she has made some real progress: she feels better about herself, she can wear clothes that hadn't fit for years, and people regularly compliment her appearance.

One Tuesday night, when alone in front of the television, Sophie had an irresistible urge for cheesecake. Once the idea had taken hold, she couldn't erase it from her mind, and the thought became unbearable. Her diet allowed for dessert only once a week, and she had already eaten her quota. She tried not to think about it, but the idea of a nice piece of cheesecake (with raspberry topping) haunted her, and she wanted nothing more than to go to a restaurant, sit down, and ask for some.

1. At this point, what steps could Sophie take to avoid a relapse?

_____

_____

_____

_____

_____

_____

2. What might she say to herself to help avoid a relapse?

_____

_____

_____

_____

_____

Unfortunately, while Sophie was trying to resist the urge for cheesecake, she saw a Sara Lee commercial. The timing was too much: she got up and headed to the nearest grocery store. On the way, she felt guilty, but put such thoughts out of mind. Once there, she decided to buy a family-size New York-style cheesecake along with two pints of milk, and she returned quickly home to devour it all. After she finished eating, Sophie felt sick and guilty. She was despondent and regretted giving in to her urge.

3. If you were in Sophie's place after exceeding your limit, what would you do?

    a) I would tell myself that all my efforts so far have been useless and that I'm a failure. I would head to the store to buy chocolate (since I am relapsing, what's the difference?).

    b) I would tell myself that a single slip does not erase all my efforts to date. I would try to figure out why I failed to resist this one urge, and plan how to deal with similar ones in the future. Then, I would continue with my eating limits and exercises the next day.

From this story, what do you think is the best way to react should you exceed your limits?

1) _____

2) _____

3) _____

4) _____

Tip

If you find yourself breaking your gambling limits on a particular occasion, try viewing it as a *slip* rather than a relapse. People often experience slips when trying to change well-established habits. The trick to managing them is:

- First, define them as slips (not full-blown relapses).

- Second, shift your thinking to what you might do differently if similar circumstances occur in the future.

4. If you were to experience a relapse or a slip, what do you imagine it would look like?

_____

_____

_____

_____

5. Have you experienced a relapse/slip in the past? YES ____ NO ____

If YES, briefly describe *one* and how you dealt with it (include a description of the high-risk situation and the thoughts that led to it).

_____

_____

_____

_____

6. What do you think would most likely cause you to relapse over the next 6 months?

_____

_____

_____

_____

7. List some steps you might take to help avoid experiencing a relapse.

a) _____

b) _____

c) _____

d) _____

e) _____

f) _____

Relapse Warning Signs

As indicated, it is common for people to slip when they are trying to change well-established habits. Occasionally exceeding your limits is known as a slip; going back to your original patterns of gambling is a relapse. Being aware of when you are more likely to slip or relapse is a key to prevention. The following signs often indicate that you are in danger of a slip or relapse:

1. I am starting to react too much to stress.

2. My friends and/or family are irritating me.

3. I am distancing myself from my spouse, my family, my friends, my work, and so forth.

4. I am feeling overwhelmed by loneliness, frustration, anger, and stress.

5. I get angry too easily.

6. I am starting to cut myself off from others.

7. I feel depressed a lot of the time.

8. I'm no longer able to get myself interested in anything.

9. I find myself living mostly in the past or in the future.

10. I daydream about how good things were in the past.

11. I am going through periods of confusion, not knowing what to do or think.

12. I find myself blaming other people and circumstances for my problems.

13. I find myself complaining about my fate, and feel like I'm a victim of it.

14. My daily habits are deteriorating: irregular sleep (too much/not enough), work (overwhelming/not engaging), and difficulty getting up for my usual activities.

15. I am resisting going for help and talking about dealing with my problems.

16. I sometimes wonder if returning to heavy gambling would be so bad, because things are already unbearable.

17. I am starting to consciously lie to people.

18. I am starting to use more medication, alcohol, or drugs than usual.

19. I am starting to spend time with friends who encourage heavy gambling.

20. I am starting to tell myself that I am cured and am above my problems of the past.

21. I have instigated/am going through major change (e.g., loss, deception, grief, job).

22. I am becoming overly confident and losing sight of what I have learned in therapy.

If you are experiencing one or more of these signs, take preventive action. Take time to analyze what is happening and how it can lead to heavy gambling and problems. Try to apply your two key strategies:

▪ Avoid high-risk situations.

▪ Identify and correct your erroneous thoughts regarding gambling.

If these strategies don't seem to work, contact your therapist.

Emergency Measures Part I: Preventing a Slip

Stay Calm!

Often, the first reaction to an urge or temptation to gamble heavily is to doubt whether you can resist it. This is normal and is not dangerous unless you allow yourself to follow through and give up control. The key is to keep control by regaining your calm and focus. Here are some steps to follow.

Step 1

Give yourself time: allow the temptation or urge to fully "arrive" and then "depart."

Picture it as a wave on the ocean: it builds, reaches its peak, breaks, and subsides. This is exactly what happens to urges and temptations: if you do not respond, chances are they will disappear after a while.

Step 2

Describe the urges or temptations you are feeling; put them into words in your mind. Consider them as "wild horses" that want you to charge into old habits.

Step 3

Ask yourself, "What's my bottom line?" How important is it to get your gambling under control? Recall that you are the one who chooses where to go. Make your choice.

Step 4

Go over the emergency card provided on page 71.

When experiencing these urges and temptations, it is always more difficult to keep your head "cold." By definition, they move you into a "hot" state of mind. Giving yourself breathing space helps cool things down and allows you to refocus on your goals and why you adopted them in the first place.

Key Insight

Each time you resist an urge or temptation to gamble too much, you weaken its power. This is why it is hardest to do the first time you try. But once you succeed the first time, the second will be a little less difficult, and the third less difficult again. Over time, resisting the urges and temptations to exceed your limits becomes your new pattern of behavior and your key resource for success.

Emergency Measures Part 2: Managing a Slip

The Myth of Instant Perfection

People who are trying to cut back on their gambling often find themselves in situations where they have exceeded their limits, either by playing too long or spending too much. Often, their first reaction is to feel guilty and blame themselves for giving in to the heat of the moment. Some go further and interpret the event as a sign of failure: they are tempted to abandon their efforts at control and to return to heavy gambling.

These are normal reactions and are not dangerous unless you allow yourself to follow through and let go of all control. It takes *skill* to deal with such thoughts and get back on track for your goal of controlled, problem-free gambling. This reading outlines some of the skills you can use to "manage" experiences where you exceed your limits. There are two principal types of skill:

  New ways of thinking about the experience so that it becomes a part of your learning process

New ways of acting as a result of the experience so that it is less likely to occur again in the future

The following key skills can help you better understand your slips and prepare yourself for managing them in the future.

1. Avoid Labeling Yourself as a Failure

A single episode of exceeding your limits cannot be considered a failure. It does not mean that you have no willpower, that you are failing, or that your situation is hopeless. It is about a single event that you can avoid in the future. The most constructive interpretation is to see it as an opportunity to learn from a mistake.

2. Reinforce Your Commitment

Recognize that maintaining your motivation is the priority. You may feel like abandoning everything in the belief that you have ruined it all. Again, this is a normal reaction. To counter these feelings, try the following:

- **Recall your bottom line:** Go over your reasons for cutting back on gambling, the exercise on the advantages and disadvantages of gambling and cutting back, and the long-term benefits of such a change. Ask yourself: Are these worth abandoning because you run into difficulty?

- **Have a discussion with yourself:** Recognize the one part of you that wants to cut back on gambling and the other that wants to "lay down and surrender." Remember that you are changing your habits *first and foremost for yourself*, and ask which part will prevail. This is a way of taking care of yourself and your life.

- **Review your efforts so far:** Recognize the progress you have made to date. Think about the times when you had the urge to exceed your limits and successfully resisted. Ask yourself what helped you most on those occasions.

- **Reframe the event:** People who succeed see setbacks as "slips" on the path to their goal. A slip is part of any difficult change process. Resolve to learn what you can from it and get back on course.

3. Analyze Your Slip

Rather than giving in to feeling guilty for what has happened, choose a course that makes it easier to react effectively.

▪ **Review the slip:**

Where were you? _____

What was happening? _____

What was the time of day? _____

Who was with you? _____

What was your mood? _____

What were you doing when the urge to gamble intensified?

_____

Which thoughts started and fed your urge to gamble? _____

_____

Which thoughts "gave you permission" to exceed your limits?

_____

Were there warning signs before the slip? If so, what were they?

_____

Each of these questions gives you important information about the thoughts, feelings, and circumstances that got you into trouble. You will need to react differently to them in the future.

▪ **Review your efforts to control the slip:**

A. If you attempted to do something before the slip:

Which strategy did you use to counter the urge to gamble?

_____

Why didn't it work? _____

_____

B. If you didn't try anything before the slip:

Why not? _____

_____

Has your motivation diminished? If so, why? _____

_____

_____

▦ **Plan for the future:**

Imagine that the same circumstances that resulted in your slip are repeated. Imagine also that you are stronger and more capable of managing it effectively.

What could you do the next time to be more effective? _____

_____

New ways of thinking: _____

_____

_____

New ways of acting: _____

_____

_____

4. Ask for Help

If you feel you have done all you can and still are unable to pinpoint what caused the slip, ask for help. Whether it is with a friend, a support agency, or a therapist, take steps to engage someone else. A second set of "interested eyes" can help you assess what happened and identify a broader set of options to consider.

The driver who has a flat tire and can't repair it does not hesitate to flag down a vehicle or call a mechanic for help. Do like this driver, and give yourself permission to ask for help.

MEMORY AID

When facing overwhelming urges or a slip:

1. I stay calm; I distance myself and reflect on what just happened.

2. I identify the thoughts that tell me to exceed my limits.

3. I recall the principles of chance:
   - It gives a false impression about the likelihood of winning.
   - Results are unpredictable.
   - Each play is independent.
   - No strategy works; there is no way to control the outcome.
   - Negative expected winnings = more to lose than to win

4. I remember all the effort I have invested so far.

5. I remember all the advantages of controlling my gambling.

6. I ask for help from others if all of the above fail.

Photocopy this page and keep it in your wallet or purse for easy access in case of emergency. You may also download a copy from the Treatments *ThatWork*™ Web site at www.oup.com/us/ttw.

Homework

(To be done between sessions 11 and 12)

✎ Review the following workbook materials:

Relapse Prevention: Sophie's Relapse

Relapse Warning Signs

Emergency Measures Part 1: Preventing a Slip

Memory Aid

✎ Continue applying strategies to avoid/manage high-risk situations.

✎ If needed, continue practicing problem-solving skills.

✎ Continue to complete the Daily Self-Monitoring Diary.

Chapter 9   *Posttreatment Assessment*

Goals

▪ To complete assessment questionnaires on pages 74 and 75.

Posttreatment Assessment

Now that you have finished the program, your therapist will work with you to complete the questionnaires that were introduced during your pretreatment assessment (see Chapter 2).

Diagnostic Interview for Pathological Gambling

Once again your therapist will begin your assessment by asking you a number of questions from the Diagnostic Interview for Pathological Gambling (DIPG).

Gambling-Related Questions

For questions 1 and 2, circle the number that corresponds to the way that you have felt over the past week.

Perceived Control

1. To what extent do you feel that your gambling problem is resolved or under control?

0 ----- 10 ----- 20 ----- 30 ----- 40 ----- 50 ----- 60 ----- 70 ----- 80 ----- 90 ----- 100%

| Not at all resolved | A little | Moderately | A lot | Totally resolved |

Urge to Gamble

2. To what extent have you felt the urge to gamble in the past week?

0 ----- 10 ----- 20 ----- 30 ----- 40 ----- 50 ----- 60 ----- 70 ----- 80 ----- 90 ----- 100%

| Not at all | A little | Moderately | A lot | Totally |

Gambling Frequency

3. How many times have you gambled in the past week? _____

4. How much time (hours and minutes) have you spent gambling during the past week? _____

5. How much money have you wagered during the past week? _____

Perceived Self-Efficacy Questionnaire

Please describe your high-risk situations for gambling excessively (for example: "when I am bored and have nothing to do" or "when I just had an argument with my boss"). Then, indicate on a scale of 0 to 10 your level of confidence in controlling your gambling habits if you faced these situations at the present time.

Situation 1

_____

_____

_____

If you had to face this situation at the present time, to what extent would you have confidence in controlling your gambling habits?

0 ------- 1 ------- 2 ------- 3 ------- 4 ------- 5 ------- 6 ------- 7 ------- 8 ------- 9 ------- 10

Not at all   A little   Moderately   A lot   Totally

Situation 2

_____

_____

_____

If you had to face this situation at the present time, to what extent would you have confidence in controlling your gambling habits?

0 ------- 1 ------- 2 ------- 3 ------- 4 ------- 5 ------- 6 ------- 7 ------- 8 ------- 9 ------- 10

Not at all   A little   Moderately   A lot   Totally

Situation 3

_____

_____

_____

If you had to face this situation at the present time, to what extent would you have confidence in controlling your gambling habits?

0 ------- 1 ------- 2 ------- 3 ------- 4 ------- 5 ------- 6 ------- 7 ------- 8 ------- 9 ------- 10

Not at all   A little   Moderately   A lot   Totally

The measures included in this chapter will help you and your therapist determine whether or not a behavioral change has occurred as a result of treatment. Have you reduced or altogether stopped your gambling behaviors? If so, has this change led to a reduction or fading of the negative consequences associated with your gambling? Your therapist will discuss the results of your posttreatment assessment with you.

Chapter 10   *Follow-Up Assessment*

Goals

▦ To attend follow-up sessions with your therapist over the next several months to make sure you're still "on track"

▦ To complete assessments to measure progress that was made during treatment

Diagnostic Interview for Pathological Gambling

Your therapist will administer the Diagnostic Interview for Pathological Gambling (DIPG) one final time. You will also complete the Gambling-Related Questions and Perceived Self-Efficacy questionnaires (on pages 78 and 79) again.

Gambling-Related Questions

For questions 1 and 2, circle the number that corresponds to the way that you have felt over the past week.

Perceived Control

1. To what extent do you feel that your gambling problem is resolved or under control?

0 ----- 10 ----- 20 ----- 30 ----- 40 ----- 50 ----- 60 ----- 70 ----- 80 ----- 90 ----- 100%

| Not at all resolved | A little | Moderately | A lot | Totally resolved |

Urge to Gamble

2. To what extent have you felt the urge to gamble in the past week?

0 ----- 10 ----- 20 ----- 30 ----- 40 ----- 50 ----- 60 ----- 70 ----- 80 ----- 90 ----- 100%

| Not at all | A little | Moderately | A lot | Totally |

Gambling Frequency

3. How many times have you gambled in the past week? _____

4. How much time (hours and minutes) have you spent gambling during the past week? _____

5. How much money have you wagered during the past week? _____

Perceived Self-Efficacy Questionnaire

Please describe your high-risk situations for gambling excessively (for example: "when I am bored and have nothing to do" or "when I just had an argument with my boss"). Then, indicate on a scale of 0 to 10 your level of confidence in controlling your gambling habits if you faced these situations at the present time.

Situation 1

_____

_____

_____

If you had to face this situation at the present time, to what extent would you have confidence in controlling your gambling habits?

0 ------- 1 ------- 2 ------- 3 ------- 4 ------- 5 ------- 6 ------- 7 ------- 8 ------- 9 ------- 10

Not at all   A little   Moderately   A lot   Totally

Situation 2

_____

_____

_____

If you had to face this situation at the present time, to what extent would you have confidence in controlling your gambling habits?

0 ------- 1 ------- 2 ------- 3 ------- 4 ------- 5 ------- 6 ------- 7 ------- 8 ------- 9 ------- 10

Not at all   A little   Moderately   A lot   Totally

Situation 3

_____

_____

_____

If you had to face this situation at the present time, to what extent would you have confidence in controlling your gambling habits?

0 ------- 1 ------- 2 ------- 3 ------- 4 ------- 5 ------- 6 ------- 7 ------- 8 ------- 9 ------- 10

Not at all   A little   Moderately   A lot   Totally

Congratulations! You are well on your way to overcoming your gambling problem. With patience and continued effort, you will be able to maintain your progress and make even more gains. Keep in mind that you have vulnerabilities that led to your gambling in the first place. These emotional and behavioral habits are part of you, but like most people, you can overcome them so you have control over your behavior.

References

American Psychiatric Association (1994). *Diagnostic and statistical manual of mental disorders* (4th ed.). Washington DC: American Psychiatric Association.

Beaudoin, C., & Cox, B. (1999). Characteristics of problem gambling in a Canadian context: a preliminary study using a DSM-IV-based questionnaire. *Canadian Journal of Psychiatry, 44,* 483–487.

Beconia, E. (1992). Prevalence surveys of problem and pathological gambling in Europe: the cases of Germany, Holland and Spain. *Journal of Gambling Studies, 12,* 179–192.

Blaszczynski, A., & McConaghy, N. (1993). A two- to nine-year follow-up study of pathological gambling. In W. Eadington (Ed.), *Gambling behavior and problem gambling.* Institute for the Study of Gambling and Commercial Gaming, University of Nevada, Reno.

Blaszczynski, A., McConaghy, N., & Frankova, A. (1991). Control versus abstinence in the treatment of pathological gambling: a two- to nine-year follow-up. *British Journal of Addictions, 86,* 299–306.

Crockford, D. N., & el-Guebaly, N. (1998). Psychiatric comorbidity in pathological gambling: a critical review. *Canadian Journal of Psychiatry, 43,* 43–50.

Ladouceur, R. (1996). The prevalence of pathological gambling in Canada. *Journal of Gambling Studies, 12,* 129–142.

Ladouceur, R. (2004). Perceptions among pathological and non-pathological gamblers. *Addictive Behaviors, 29,* 555–565.

Ladouceur, R., Jacques, C., Chevalier, S., Sévigny, S., & Hamel, D. (2005). Prevalence of pathological gambling in Quebec in 2002. *Canadian Journal of Psychiatry, 50,* 451–456.

Ladouceur, R., Sylvain, C., Boutin, C., & Doucet, C. (2000). *Le jeu excessif: comprendre et vaincre le gambling.* Montréal: Les Éditions de l'Homme.

Ladouceur, R., Sylvain, C., Boutin, C., & Doucet, C. (2002). *Understanding and treating pathological gamblers.* London: Wiley.

Ladouceur, R., Sylvain, C., Boutin, C., Lachance, S., Doucet, C., Leblond, J., & Jacques, C. (2001). Cognitive treatment of pathological gambling. *Journal of Nervous and Mental Disease, 189,* 766–773.

Lejoyeux, M., Feuche, L., Loi, S., Solomon, J., & Ades, J. (1999). Study of impulsive control among alcohol-dependent patients. *Journal of Clinical Psychiatry, 60,* 302–305.

Linden, R. D., Pope, H. G., & Jonas, J. M. (1986). Pathological gambling and major affective disorder: preliminary findings. *Journal of Clinical Psychiatry, 47,* 201–203.

Marlatt, G. A., & Gordon, J. R. (Ed.). (1985). *Relapse prevention: maintenance strategies in the treatment of addictive behaviors.* New York: Guilford Press.

McCormick, R. A., Russo, A. M., Ramirez, L. F., & Taber, J. I. (1984). Affective disorders among pathological gamblers seeking treatment. *American Journal of Psychiatry, 141,* 215–218.

Miller, W. R. (1983). Motivational interviewing with problem drinkers. *Behavioural Psychotherapy, 11,* 147–172.

Miller, W. R., Benefield, R. G., & Tonigan, J. S. (1993). Enhancing motivation for change in problem drinking: a controlled comparison of two therapist styles. *Journal of Consulting and Clinical Psychology, 61,* 455–461.

Miller, W. R., & Rollnick, S. (1991). *Motivational interviewing: preparing people to change addictive behavior.* New York: Guilford Press.

Najavits, L. M. (2003). How to design an effective treatment outcome study. *Journal of Gambling Studies, 19,* 278–337.

National Gambling Impact Study Commission (1999). *Final report.* Washington DC: Government Printing Office.

Shaffer, H. J., Hall, M. N., & VanderBilt, J. (1997). Estimating the prevalence of disordered gambling behavior in the United States and Canada: a research synthesis. *American Journal of Public Health, 89,* 1369–1376.

Smart, R. G., & Ferris, J. (1996). Alcohol, drugs and gambling in the Ontario adult population. *Canadian Journal of Psychiatry, 41,* 36–45.

Sylvain, C., Ladouceur, R., & Boisvert, J.-M. (1997). Cognitive and behavioral treatment of pathological gambling: a controlled study. *Journal of Consulting and Clinical Psychology, 65,* 727–732.

Toneatto, T., & Ladouceur, R. (2003). The treatment of pathological gambling: a critical review of the literature. *Psychology of Addictive Behaviors, 17,* 284–292.

About the Authors

Robert Ladouceur is full professor in psychology at Laval University, Quebec, Canada, and a licensed clinical psychologist in the Province of Quebec. He is also the director of the Centre d'excellence pour la prevention et le traitement du jeu, a group of 20 researchers and clinicians working on different issues related to gambling (epidemiology, prevention, treatment, and the fundamental aspects of gambling behavior). He has published over 150 articles and chapters in the areas of gambling. His work on gambling is internationally known. He was invited twice to present his work at the National Gambling Impact Study Commission, the U.S. Presidential Commission on Gambling. In 1996, he received the Research Award from the National Council on Problem Gambling, recognizing the high quality of his work. In 2003, he received the Senior Research Award from the National Center for Responsible Gaming, Harvard University.

He has presented his work in many Canadian provinces, American states, and European and Asian countries. His cognitive treatment for pathological gamblers developed at Laval University is widely used. He recently published a paper on responsible gambling called the Reno Model with Alex Blaszczynski from the University of Sydney, Australia, and Howard Shaffer from Harvard University.

Stella Lachance is a psychologist who has worked at the Center of Excellence for the Prevention and Treatment of Problem Gambling at Laval University since 1996. As a clinician-researcher, she has been extensively involved in the development and delivery of treatment for pathological gambling and has provided therapy to many gamblers over the years. In addition, she contributed to the development of a step-by-step treatment guide for problem gamblers, which has been endorsed by the Quebec Ministry of Health and Social Services and is used by most treatment centers in the Province of Quebec. Since 2000, she has conducted many workshops, presented at conferences, and provided numerous training sessions on the treatment of problem gambling.

CPSIA information can be obtained at www.ICGtesting.com
Printed in the USA
LVOW09s1414180114

369973LV00004B/36/P